Find the Nutcracker

in His Christmas Ballet

Illustrated by Jerry Tiritilli

Louis Weber, C.E.O.
Publications International, Ltd.
7373 North Cicero Avenue
Lincolnwood, Illinois 60646

Permission is never granted for commercial purposes.

Manufactured in the U.S.A.

8 7 6 5 4 3 2

ISBN 1-56173-163-3

PUBLICATIONS INTERNATIONAL, LTD.

When the ballet opens, it is Christmas Eve at Fritz and Marie's house. Family and friends have gathered to share the joys of the season. Godfather Drosselmeier has brought the children a special present—a nutcracker he has made himself. Naughty Fritz broke the nutcracker while trying to crack a very hard nut!

Can you find the children and their Christmas gifts?

Nutcracker

Marie

Fritz

Marie's doll, Clara

Six toy soldiers

Five golden walnuts

A hobby horse

A clown doll

Late that night when Marie crept downstairs to check on Nutcracker, a fierce battle was raging between Fritz's toy soldiers and the mice! Marie threw her slipper at the Mouse King. She saved Nutcracker's life and helped win the battle!

Can you find the brave Nutcracker? Can you find these other brave soldiers, too?

Sergeant Whiskers

Corporal Cliff Dover

Hugh of the Highlands

Admiral Blownapart

General Steadfast

Private Beauregard

Ace Von Cheddar

Dartanian, a "mouseketeer"

When Marie defeated the Mouse King, she broke the spell that had turned a handsome prince into a nutcracker. Prince Nutcracker invited Marie to join him on a Christmas journey in his magic sleigh. The sleigh took them through the Christmas Woods where Snow Fairies danced in the moonlight.

Do you see Prince Nutcracker?

Can you find these animals hiding in the Christmas Woods?

A dove

A polar bear

An arctic fox

A penguin

A snowy owl

A unicorn

A white mouse

Next, the magic sleigh took Marie and Prince Nutcracker to the Land of Sweets. The Sugar Plum Fairy and all her subjects were there to greet them. Some of Marie's friends from other scenes are enjoying the Land of Sweets, too.

Can you find Marie's friends? You must also help one little angel find her toe-shoe ribbons. Don't forget to look for Prince Nutcracker!

Prince Nutcracker

Marie

The Snow Queen

Three little angels with golden wings

The marzipan shepherdess

Three cotton-candy sheep

Lost ribbons from a pair of toe shoes

The Sugar Plum Fairy clapped her hands. All at once, they were in Spain! Spanish dancers performed a dance about chocolate for Marie and Prince Nutcracker. Everywhere she looked, Marie saw rich, dark chocolate. She also saw many wonderful Spanish things that she had never seen before.

Can you find these Spanish things? Can you find Prince Nutcracker, too?

A matador

This bull

Señor Flamenco

Señora Flamenco

This pretty fan

This burro

This guitar

Three galleons

These castanets

Next, Marie and Prince Nutcracker found themselves in the middle of an Arabian marketplace where dancers performed a dance about coffee. There were many wonderful sights and sounds, but best of all was the smell of roasted coffee beans in the air.

Can you find these Arabian things? Remember to look for Prince Nutcracker, too!

An Arabian horse

Sindbad the Sailor

Aladdin's lamp

A genie

This magic carpet

Ali Baba

This camel

A cup of coffee

This shepherd

As soon as the Arabian coffee dancers finished their dance, Marie and Prince Nutcracker were whisked away to snowy Russia! There, in the town square, Russian cossacks leapt and twirled and danced for their guests of honor. Marie was thrilled with the lively music and dancing!

Look for Prince Nutcracker first. Then look for these Russian things.

The hammer & sickle

Ivan the Terrible

A balalaika

A circus bear

A fiddler

A Bolshoi ballerina

Matreshkas

A Ukrainian egg

Marie had grown chilly, so she asked for a cup of hot tea. At once, she was in China where acrobats tumbled and turned in a wonderful tea dance! Marie clapped her hands in delight as the acrobats performed one amazing feat after another.

Can you find these Chinese things in this scene? Prince Nutcracker is hiding here, too.

A sharpei puppy

A dragon kite

A paper lantern

Chinese checkers

A gong

A pair of chopsticks

A China doll

A panda bear

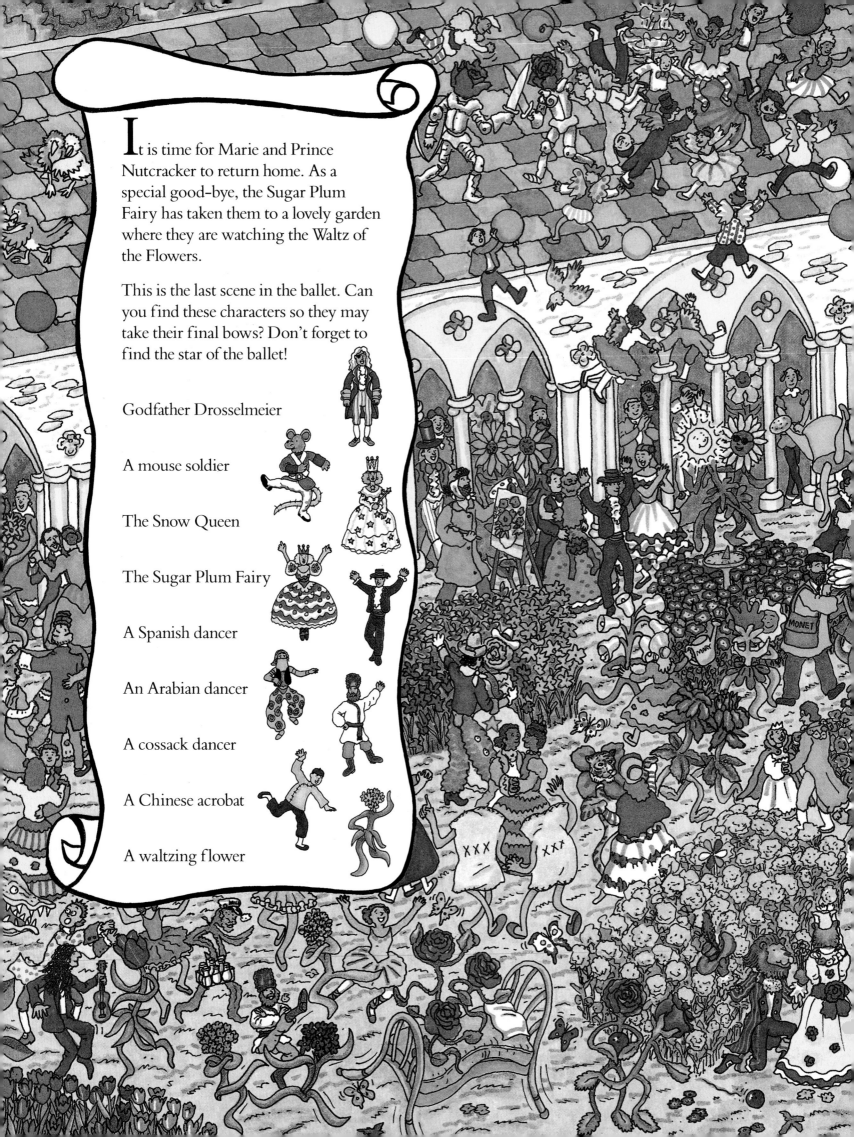

It is time for Marie and Prince Nutcracker to return home. As a special good-bye, the Sugar Plum Fairy has taken them to a lovely garden where they are watching the Waltz of the Flowers.

This is the last scene in the ballet. Can you find these characters so they may take their final bows? Don't forget to find the star of the ballet!

Godfather Drosselmeier

A mouse soldier

The Snow Queen

The Sugar Plum Fairy

A Spanish dancer

An Arabian dancer

A cossack dancer

A Chinese acrobat

A waltzing flower

Turn back to the opening scene of the ballet. Can you find these things?

☐ An electric fan
☐ A human hat rack
☐ A mouse taking the cake
☐ A *very* warm kitty
☐ Someone roasting a hot dog
☐ A poor match under the mistletoe
☐ A "toast"
☐ Marie's missing slipper

Look for these "cool" things in the Christmas Woods.

☐ Ice cream
☐ Ice hockey
☐ Ice cubes
☐ Iceberg
☐ Iced tea
☐ Icicle
☐ Ice bucket
☐ Icebox

Did you see these funny things when you were in the Land of Sweets?

☐ A mid-air collision
☐ A candy-cane snorkeler
☐ The Tooth Fairy
☐ A jelly-bean garden
☐ The Gingerbread Man running as fast as he can
☐ A spoonful of sugar
☐ A pickle
☐ A bubble-gum ball game

Look for these mouse and rat sayings in the Battle scene.

☐ "I smell a rat!"
☐ "Rat race"
☐ "Quiet as a church mouse"
☐ "You dirty rat!"
☐ "The mouse ran up the clock"
☐ "Three Blind Mice"
☐ "A better mousetrap"

Go back to Spain to find these chocolate things.

☐ A chocolate moose
☐ A chocolate bunny with one ear bitten off
☐ Chocolate chips
☐ A chocolate ice-cream cone
☐ A chocolate pie
☐ A chocoholic
☐ A chocolate cake
☐ A cup of hot chocolate